WITHDRAWN

THE INFERNAL DEVICES
CLOCKWORK PRINCE

CHAPTER 9

HALLO, MOL. YOU'RE LOOKING PARTICULARLY FINE THIS EVENING, IF I DO SAY SO.

I NEED FORAII DEMON POWDERS, GROUND FINE.

NOW WHAT'S A FINE YOUNG MAN LIKE YOU WANT WITH STUFF LIKE THAT?

WILLIAM 'ERONDALE. BACK AGAIN SO SOON?

DON'T TRY TO BARGAIN. I'LL GIVE YOU A GOOD PRICE.

THESE ALL FIT YOUR DESCRIPTION, MOL.

ALTHOUGH I DOUBT THAT HER WEDDING RING IS AMONG THEM.

FOR ME...

I'VE BECOME VERY FOND OF JEM OVER THE PAST FORTNIGHT.

SO THIS IS WESTMINSTER ABBEY?

WILL HAS BEEN STUDIOUSLY AVOIDING ME, CHARLOTTE AND HENRY HAVE BEEN CAUGHT UP IN ISSUES OF CLAVE AND COUNCIL AND THE RUNNING OF THE INSTITUTE—AND EVEN JESSAMINE HAS SEEMED PREOCCUPIED.

POETS' CORNER.

HENRY JAMES
OM
Novelist
New York 1843
London 1916

THOMAS STEARNS
ELIOT
OM
BORN 26 SEPTEMBER 1888
DIED 4 JANUARY 1965

I KNOW WE ARE IN A HURRY TO GET TO THE COUNCIL MEETING, BUT I WANTED YOU TO SEE THIS.

BUT JEM WAS ALWAYS THERE.

I NEVER SAID I WASN'T COMING.

......

WELL, LET'S HURRY. WE'RE LATE.

THE CONSUL. HE'S— THE HEAD OF THE CLAVE? LIKE A SORT OF KING?

YOU' SEE SOO ENOU

THESE FOUR C'S STAND FOR CLAVE AND COUNCIL, COVENANT AND CONSUL.

NOT QUITE SO INBRED AS YOUR USUAL MONARCH— HE'S ELECTED.

MR. HERONDALE, MR. CARSTAIRS, HOW KIND OF YOU TO JOIN US.

MISS THERESA GRAY OF NEW YORK.

AND YOUR COMPANION MUST BE—

HOW COULD SHE INTERRUPT THE CONSUL?!

MURMUR

MURMUR

WELCOME, THEN, MISS TESSA GRAY OF NEW YORK.

I UNDERSTAND YOU HAVE ALREADY ANSWERED QUITE A FEW QUESTIONS FOR THE LONDON ENCLAVE. I HAD HOPED YOU WOULD BE WILLING TO ANSWER A FEW MORE.

IF THAT IS YOUR REQUEST, CERTAINLY.

THIS IS THE GARD COUNCIL. WE DON'T BRING DOWNWORLDERS TO THIS PLACE.

PATIENCE, BENEDICT.

SHE SHOULDN'T BE HERE!

WE ARE NOT GOING TO HURT YOU, LITTLE WARLOCK.

YOU SHOULD NOT CALL ME WARLOCK.

I BEAR NO WARLOCK'S MARK.

SHE MAY BE ALLOWED TO GIVE EVIDENCE, BUT HER TESTIMONY WILL BE COUNTED ONLY AS HALF A SHADOW-HUNTER'S.

YES. HER PARENTS AND BROTHER WERE HUMAN AS WELL.

IT IS TRUE?

MOST CURIOUS, EVERYTHING ABOUT YOU, INCLUDING THIS POWER OF YOURS. HAVE YOU BEEN TESTED WITH AN ITEM OF MORTMAIN'S?

YES, I...TRIED. WITH A BUTTON HE HAD LEFT BEHIND. BUT I COULD NOT DO IT.

WE HAVE SEARCHED EVERYWHERE, BUT THE MAN HAS VANISHED.

......

FIND MORTMAIN? ALONE, JUST HENRY AND I— WITH NO HELP FROM THE REST OF THE ENCLAVE?

YOU MAY ASK FOR HELP IF YOU HAVE SOME SPECIFIC NEED. BUT AS FOR THE INVESTIGATION, YES, THAT IS FOR YOU TO ACCOMPLISH ON YOUR OWN.

BUT WE HAVE JUST LOST OUR SERVANTS.

NEW SERVANTS WILL BE PROVIDED TO YOU, AS IS STANDARD. WELL-TRAINED FIGHTERS.

NOT ONLY IS MISS LOVELACE BEHIND IN HER TRAINING, BUT YOUR PARLOR GIRL, SOPHIE, AND THAT DOWNWORLDER THERE... IT WOULD HARDLY HURT IF SHE AND THE MAID WERE TRAINED IN THE BASICS OF DEFENSE.

IS HE TALKING ABOUT ME?!

SINCE THE TWO OF YOU WILL BE BUSY INVESTIGATING, I SUGGEST I LEND YOU MY SONS— GABRIEL AND GIDEON— AS TRAINERS.

WE CAN TRAIN OUR OWN SERVANTS.

BENEDICT LIGHT-WOOD IS OFFERING YOU A GENEROUS GIFT. ACCEPT IT.

IF YOU CONSIDER IT IMPOSSIBLE, THEN PERHAPS YOU SHOULD ASK YOURSELF WHY YOU WANT THE JOB SO BADLY IN THE FIRST PLACE.

CHARLOTTE, I THINK WE'RE WASTING OUR TIME.

WE KNOW MORTMAIN'S PAST, AND HIS PLANS. BORN IN DEVON, WAS A SHIP'S SURGEON, BECAME A WEALTHY TRADER, GOT HIMSELF MIXED UP IN DARK MAGIC...

BUT WHAT WE WANT TO KNOW IS WHERE HE LEARNED DARK MAGIC, AND FROM WHOM.

AND WHY HE HATES SHADOW-HUNTERS.

IS IT HATRED? I ASSUMED IT WAS A SIMPLE GREED FOR DOMINATION.

NO, HE HATES THE NEPHILIM. IT IS SOMETHING VERY PERSONAL FOR HIM.

IT'S AS IF HE DESIRES RECOMPENSE FOR SOME WRONG OR HURT THEY'VE DONE HIM.

REPARATIONS.

WHEN A DOWNWORLDER, OR A MUNDANE, ALLEGES THAT A SHADOWHUNTER HAS BROKEN THE LAW IN THEIR DEALINGS WITH THEM, THE DOWNWORLDER LODGES A COMPLAINT THROUGH REPARATIONS.

IT'S NOT LIKE MORTMAIN'S GOING TO LODGE A COMPLAINT AGAINST THE SHADOW-HUNTERS THROUGH OFFICIAL CHANNELS.

WHAT'S THE HARM IN ASKING?

I'M OFF TO CATCH CHARLOTTE BEFORE BROTHER ENOCH LEAVES AND ASK HER TO HAVE THE SILENT BROTHERS CHECK THE ARCHIVES.

I'LL GO WITH YOU, JEM.

NOT IF THEY'RE MUNDANES. SOMEONE AS PRETTY AS JESSAMINE OUGHT TO HAVE HER PICK, BUT SHE'S SO DETERMINED THAT A SHADOWHUNTER WON'T DO—

YOU ARE MUCH PRETTIER.

JESSAMINE?

KNOCK KNOCK

SHE'LL NEVER WEAR IT.

I NEVER AGREED TO WRESTLE HER INTO THE CLOTHES, JUST TO DELIVER THEM.

SLUMP

CLICK

DON'T THEY LOOK TOO HORRIBLE BY HALF?

?

I ACTUALLY RECOGNIZE A FEW FROM THE CODEX.

THAT ONE THERE'S A LONGSWORD, AND THERE'S A RAPIER, AND THAT ONE IS A CLAYMORE, I THINK.

CLOSE.

IT'S AN EXECUTIONER'S SWORD. MOSTLY FOR DECAPITATIONS.

JEM!

THE LIGHTWOODS WILL BE HERE. THEY'RE SIMPLY BEING LATE TO MAKE A POINT.

I WISH YOU WERE THE ONE TRAINING US.

I COULDN'T...

I HAVEN'T COMPLETED MY OWN TRAINING YET.

I SHOULDN'T HAVE SAID THAT. HE'S NOT WELL ENOUGH OFTEN ENOUGH TO TRAIN US RELIABLY.

AHEM.

WELL, WE'RE HERE AS WE SAID WE WOULD BE. JAMES, I ASSUME YOU REMEMBER MY BROTHER, GIDEON. MISS GRAY, MISS COLLINS—

WHEN DID YOU GET BACK FROM MADRID?

FATHER CALLED ME BACK HOME A SHORT WHILE AGO. FAMILY BUSINESS.

NOW, BEFORE WE MOVE TO THE TRAINING PORTION OF THIS VISIT, THERE ARE TWO PEOPLE YOU SHOULD PROBABLY MEET.

MR. TANNER...

THOMAS!

...AND MISS DALY.

I'M THOMAS'S BROTHER, MISS. CYRIL. CYRIL TANNER.

CYRIL WILL REPLACE THOMAS, AND BRIDGET WILL REPLACE YOUR LOST COOK, AGATHA.

THEY WERE BOTH TRAINED IN FINE SHADOWHUNTER HOUSEHOLDS.

NO ONE COULD REPLACE AGATHA OR THOMAS FOR US, GABRIEL.

...WOULD YOU LIKE A DEMONSTRATION?

CYRIL.

YES?

THE GIRLS MIGHT AS WELL SEE THAT A MUNDANE CAN FIGHT ALMOST LIKE A SHADOW-HUNTER, WITH THE RIGHT KIND OF INSTRUCTION.

WE ALREADY KNOW THAT. THOMAS AND AGATHA WERE BOTH TRAINED.

GABRIEL IS ONLY TRYING TO ANNOY YOU. DO NOT LET HIM SEE THAT HE BOTHERS YOU.

GABRIEL ISN'T A BAD TEACHER, ACTUALLY.

THE NEW GIRL CAN COOK.

TESSA, ARE YOU ALL RIGHT? IS IT THE TRAINING?

THERE'S A SALVE THE SILENT BROTHERS MAKE FOR SORE MUSCLES. KNOCK ON THE DOOR OF MY ROOM BEFORE YOU GO TO SLEEP, AND I'LL GIVE YOU SOME.

MUCH OBLIGED.

I WILL.

BAM

I FOUND IT! JEM WAS RIGHT!

THE REPARATIONS— A REQUEST FOR RECOMPENSE SENT TO THE YORK INSTITUTE IN THE NAME OF AXEL HOLLINGWORTH MORTMAIN!

IT'S SEEKING REPARATIONS FOR THE UNJUSTIFIED DEATH OF HIS PARENTS, JOHN THADDEUS AND ANNE EVELYN SHADE, ALMOST A DECADE BEFORE.

HE WAS ASKING NOT FOR MONEY BUT FOR THE GUILTY PARTIES— SHADOWHUNTERS— TO BE TRIED AND PUNISHED.

BUT THE TRIAL WAS REFUSED. THE FULL PAPERS WOULD STILL BE IN THE YORK INSTITUTE. I MUST GO AND WRITE A LETTER TO ALOYSIUS STARKWEATHER.

WHAT ARE YOU LOOKING FOR?

WILL...

IF YOU WISH TO USE THE LIBRARY, YOU MOST CERTAINLY MAY. I FOUND WHAT I WAS LOOKING FOR.

TESSA.

ISN'T THAT THE BOOK IN WHICH THE HERO'S SON IS CRUSHED TO DEATH BY A GIGANTIC HELMET THAT FALLS FROM THE SKY?

AND YOU SAID A TALE OF TWO CITIES—

I'D RATHER DIE THAN ADMIT I READ OTRANTO AND LOVED IT.

A TALE OF TWO CITIES...

YES, YOU SAID IT WAS SILLY.

I READ IT AGAIN, YOU KNOW, BECAUSE WE HAD TALKED ABOUT IT.

YOU WERE RIGHT. IT ISN'T SILLY AT ALL.

THERE IS TOO MUCH OF DESPAIR IN IT.

...IT IS LATE. I MUST RETIRE...I AM EXHAUSTED.

VATHEK.

IF YOU FOUND OTRANTO TO YOUR LIKING, I THINK YOU WILL ENJOY IT.

CHAPTER 10

ALOYSIUS STARKWEATHER IS THE MOST STUBBORN, HYPOCRITICAL, OBSTINATE, DEGENERATE—

IS SHE TALKING ABOUT THE HEAD OF YORK INSTITUTE?

YEAH, ALTHOUGH THE OLD CODGER'S ALMOST NINETY— WONDER IF HE REALL IS A DEGENERATE.

HE REFUSES TO SEE ME, OR HENRY.

HE SAYS HE'LL NEVER FORGIVE MY FAMILY FOR WHAT MY FATHER DID.

WELL, CAN'T YOU SEND SOMEONE ELSE?

SEND ME AND JEM.

HE ISN'T LIKELY TO TELL YOU ANYTHING IF HE KNOWS I SENT YOU.

CHARLOTTE, THERE *IS* A WAY WE COULD MAKE HIM TELL US.

IF SOMETHING OF HIS COULD BE RETRIEVED AND GIVEN TO ME, I COULD USE IT TO CHANGE INTO HIM.

AND PERHAPS ACCESS HIS MEMORIES. I COULD TELL YOU WHAT HE RECOLLECTS ABOUT MORTMAIN AND THE SHADES, IF ANYTHING AT ALL.

THEN, YOU'LL COME WITH US TO YORKSHIRE.

I WON'T KNOW IF I LIKE IT UNTIL I TRY IT, WILL I?

I'VE NEVER SWUM NAKED IN THE THAMES, BUT I KNOW I WOULDN'T LIKE IT.

BUT THINK HOW ENTERTAINING IT'D BE FOR SIGHT-SEERS.

THERE'S NO NEED FOR HER TO JOIN US ON THE DIRTY, SMOKY TRAINS. SHE WON'T LIKE IT.

ANYWAY, IT DOESN'T MATTER. I WISH TO GO, AND I SHALL. WHEN DO WE LEAVE?

ALOYSIUS ALWAYS HAD A WEAKNESS FOR A PRETTY FACE. TOO BAD I CAN'T GO, BUT IT'LL BE BETTER AT LEAST TO HAVE HER INSTEAD.

I'LL HAVE TO SEND ALOYSIUS A MESSAGE SAYING TO EXPECT YOU.

I'LL BE OFF TO TRAINING THEN. THE LIGHTWOODS MUST BE WAITING.

AHHHH.

TIME FOR BED.

SSK

VATHEK?

40

FOR TESSA GRAY, ON THE OCCASION OF BEING GIVEN A COPY OF VATHEK TO READ:

CALIPH VATHEK AND HIS DARK HORDE ARE BOUND FOR HELL, YOU WON'T BE BORED! YOUR FAITH IN ME WILL BE RESTORED—UNLESS THIS TOKEN YOU FIND UNTOWARD AND MY POOR GIFT YOU HAVE IGNORED.

WILL...

HA-HA-HA...

DID YOU BRING ANYTHING TO READ ON THE JOURNEY?

NO. I HAVEN'T COME ACROSS ANYTHING I PARTICULARLY WANTED TO READ LATELY.

PERHAPS WE SHOULD DISCUSS STRATEGY. STARKWEATHER HATES CHARLOTTE BUT KNOWS THAT SHE SENT US. SO HOW TO WORM OUR WAY INTO HIS GOOD GRACES?

HOW DID CHARLOTTE EXPLAIN MY PRESENCE?

SHE DIDN'T, REALLY. SHE JUST GAVE OUR NAMES.

PERHAPS SHE'S A GIRL WHO'S FALLEN MADLY IN LOVE WITH ME AND PERSISTS IN FOLLOWING ME WHEREVER I GO.

MY TALENT IS SHAPE-SHIFTING, WILL, NOT ACTING.

PERHAPS I SHOULD INTRODUCE TESSA AS MY FIANCÉE. WE CAN TELL MAD OLD ALOYSIUS THAT HER ASCENSION IS UNDERWAY.

ASCENSION?

WHEN A SHADOWHUNTER WISHES TO MARRY A MUNDANE—

BUT I THOUGHT THAT WAS FORBIDDEN?

CHUG CHUG

CHUG CHUG

IF THE SHADOWHUNTER IN QUESTION APPLIES TO THE CLAVE FOR AN ASCENSION FOR THEIR PARTNER, THE CLAVE IS REQUIRED TO CONSIDER IT FOR AT LEAST THREE MONTHS.

FWAAAANG

IT IS. *UNLESS* THE MORTAL CUP IS USED TO TURN THAT MUNDANE INTO A SHADOWHUNTER.

MEANWHILE, THE MUNDANE EMBARKS ON A COURSE OF STUDY TO LEARN ABOUT SHADOWHUNTER CULTURE.

IT WOULD SEEM REASONABLE THAT I BROUGHT YOU WITH ME. AS A POSSIBLE ASCENDER, YOU MIGHT WANT TO LEARN ABOUT INSTITUTES OTHER THAN THE ONE IN LONDON. WHAT DO YOU THINK?

IT'S A GOOD ONE, SAVE ONE THING.

IF SHE IS MEANT TO BE AFFIANCED TO YOU, TESSA WILL NEED A RING.

I HAD THOUGHT OF THAT.

SSK

THE CARSTAIRS FAMILY RING.

IF YOU WOULD...

CHARLOTTE DOESN'T WEAR A WEDDING RING.

I HADN'T REALIZED SHADOW-HUNTERS DID.

IT IS CUSTOMARY TO GIVE A GIRL YOUR FAMILY RING WHEN YOU BECOME ENGAGED...

...BUT THE ACTUAL WEDDING CEREMONY INVOLVES EXCHANGING RUNES INSTEAD OF RINGS.

ONE ON THE ARM, AND ONE OVER THE HEART.

"SET ME AS A SEAL UPON THINE HEART, AS A SEAL UPON THINE ARM: FOR LOVE IS STRONG AS DEATH; JEALOUSY IS CRUEL AS THE GRAVE." SONG OF SOLOMON.

"JEALOUSY IS CRUEL AS THE GRAVE"? THAT'S NOT...VERY ROMANTIC.

BUT MORE THAN THAT... TELL ME WHAT IT MEANS TO BE PARABATAI? BECAUSE THERE ISN'T MUCH ON IT IN THE CODEX.

IT IS RATHER DIFFICULT TO EXPLAIN... NOT EVERYONE HAS ONE. VERY FEW OF US, ACTUALLY, FIND ONE IN THE ALLOTTED TIME.

IT IS NOT MERELY A MATTER OF PROMISING TO GUARD EACH OTHER. YOU MUST SWEAR TO LAY DOWN YOUR LIFE FOR YOUR PARABATAI.

ONE CAN DRAW ON THE STRENGTH OF THEIR PARABATAI IN BATTLE. A RUNE PUT ON YOU BY YOUR PARABATAI IS ALWAYS MORE POTENT THAN ONE YOU PUT ON YOURSELF, OR ONE PUT ON BY ANOTHER.

BUT WHAT IF YOU DECIDE THAT YOU DON'T WANT TO BE PARABATAI ANYMORE?

CHUG CHUG CHUG CHUG

IF ONE OF US WERE TO BECOME A DOWNWORLDER OR A MUNDANE, THEN THE BINDING IS CUT.

AND OF COURSE, IF ONE OF US WERE TO DIE, THE OTHER WOULD BE FREE. BUT NOT TO CHOOSE ANOTHER PARABATAI.

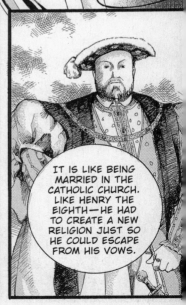

IT IS LIKE BEING MARRIED IN THE CATHOLIC CHURCH. LIKE HENRY THE EIGHTH—HE HAD TO CREATE A NEW RELIGION JUST SO HE COULD ESCAPE FROM HIS VOWS.

WELL, WILL WON'T NEED TO CREATE A NEW RELIGION JUST TO BE RID OF ME...

HE'LL BE FREE SOON ENOUGH.

I HAVEN'T ABANDONED HOPE.

I JUST HOPE FOR DIFFERENT THINGS THAN YOU DO, TESSA GRAY.

DON'T SAY THAT. A CURE COULD STILL BE FOUND. I DON'T SEE ANY REASON TO ABANDON ALL HOPE.

NEPHILIM? IS IT YOU?

AH'M 'ERE AT T'BEQUEST OF ALOYSIUS. I CAN SEE THROUGH THA' GLAMOURS, YOUNG ONES.

SAVE FOR THIS ONE. IF THERE'S A GLAMOUR ON THE GIRL, IT'S SUMMAT I'VE NEVER SEEN BEFORE.

SHE'S A MUNDANE—AN ASCENDANT. SOON TO BE MY WIFE.

...WELL, I HOPE MRS. BRANWELL TOLD ALOYSIUS SOMETHING, FOR YER SAKES.

YOUNG HERONDALE, ARE YOU? HALF-MUNDANE, HALF-WELSH, AND THE WORST TRAITS OF BOTH, I'VE HEARD.

AND JAMES CARSTAIRS. ANOTHER INSTITUTE BRAT.

I'VE HALF A MIND TO TELL THE LOT OF YOU TO GO TO BLAZES. THAT CHARLOTTE FAIRCHILD, FOISTING YOU ALL ON ME WITH NARY A BY-YOUR-LEAVE.

NONE OF THAT FAMILY EVER HAD A BIT O' MANNERS. I COULD DO WITHOUT HER FATHER, AND I CAN DO WITHOUT—

!!

THIS IS TESSA GRAY, SIR. SHE IS A MUNDANE GIRL, BUT SHE IS THE BETROTHED OF ME, AND AN ASCENDANT.

A MUNDANE, YOU SAY?

WELL, TIMES HAVE—YES, I SUPPOSE THEN—

GOTTSHALL!

YES, SIR.

GET CEDRIC AND ANDREW TO HELP YOU BRING OUR GUESTS' BELONGINGS UP TO THEIR ROOMS AND DO TELL ELLEN TO INSTRUCT COOK TO SET THREE EXTRA PLACES FOR DINNER.

HUH?

??

...AND WHERE'S OUR HOST?

WHAT ARE THOSE LIGHTNING BOLTS EVERYWHERE?

THAT IS THE STARKWEATHER FAMILY SYMBOL. IT IS BAD FORM TO BEHAVE AS IF ONE OWNS A PLACE LIKE THIS.

ONE CANNOT INHERIT AN INSTITUTE. THE GUARDIAN OF AN INSTITUTE IS APPOINTED BY THE CONSUL. THE PLACE ITSELF BELONGS TO THE CLAVE.

BUT CHARLOTTE'S PARENTS RAN THE LONDON INSTITUTE BEFORE SHE DID.

THE CONSUL WOULDN'T HAVE GIVEN CHARLOTT THE POST IF HE HADN' THOUGHT SHE WAS TH RIGHT PERSON FOR IT

THERE'S LITTLE INFORMATION ABOUT YOUR PRECIOUS MORTMAIN IN HERE.

THE BOOK SPECIALIZES IN BINDING AND UNBINDING SPELLS—TYING THE SOUL TO THE BODY, OR UNTYING IT, AS THE CASE MAY BE.

MORE ABOUT THE PARENTS. IT SEEMS SUSPICION FELL ON THEM WHEN IT WAS DISCOVERED THAT JOHN SHADE WAS IN POSSESSION OF *THE BOOK OF THE WHITE.*

TURNED OUT THE WARLOCK WAS DIGGING UP CORPSES AND REPLACING THE DAMAGED BITS WITH MECHANISMS.

THEN TRYING TO BRING THEM TO LIFE. NECROMANCY— VERY MUCH AGAINST THE LAW.

AN ENCLAVE GROUP SWEPT IN AND SLAUGHTERED BOTH WARLOCKS. BUT THE CHILD—NO HIDE NOR HAIR OF HIM.

ASSUMED HE WAS DEAD, TILL THIS TURNED UP, DEMANDING REPARATIONS.

EVEN HIS ADDRESS—

HIS ADDRESS.

THAT INFORMATION WAS NOT INCLUDED IN THE SCROLL WE SAW AT THE INSTITUTE.

IS IT IN LONDON?

NAY. RIGHT HERE IN YORKSHIRE.

RAVENSCAR MANOR. A MASSIVE OLD PILE UP NORTH FROM HERE. BEEN ABANDONED NOW, I THINK, FOR DECADES.

!!

MOST OF THE SHADES' BELONGINGS WERE TAKEN FOR SPOILS. WE'VE QUITE A COLLECTION HERE. COME ALONG. I'LL SHOW THEM TO YOU.

SPOILS! THAT'S WHERE THEY KEEP THE BELONGINGS OF A DOWN-WORLDER WHO BROKE THE LAW!

NEVER THOUGHT MUCH OF THIS REPARATIONS BUSINESS MYSELF. MAKES DOWNWORLDERS UPPITY, THINKING THEY HAVE A RIGHT TO GET SOMETHING OUT OF US.

WAS *THE BOOK OF THE WHITE* AMONG WHAT HE ASKED FOR?

MORTMAIN WAS PROTESTING THE DEATH OF ANNE SHADE—SAID SHE'D HAD NOTHING TO DO WITH HER HUSBAND'S PROJECTS, HADN'T KNOWN ABOUT THEM, HE CLAIMED.

IT WAS. IT WAS RETRIEVED AND PLACED IN THE LONDON INSTITUTE LIBRARY, WHERE NO DOUBT IT REMAINS STILL.

WERE YOU THERE?

HER DEATH WAS UNDESERVED. WANTED A TRIAL OF THOSE GUILTY OF WHAT HE CALLED HER "MURDER," AND HIS PARENTS' BELONGINGS BACK.

MORTMAIN NEVER HAD A CHANCE, DID HE. FILING HIS COMPLAINT LIKE THAT.

OF COURSE NOT!

I'D WAGER THE FATHER'D HAVE USED HIM FOR SPARE PARTS IF IT CAME DOWN TO IT. HE SHOULD HAVE BEEN THANKING US, NOT ASKING FOR A TRIAL—

......

EVER BEEN TO THE CRYSTAL PALACE?

WELL, THIS IS EVEN BETTER.

CREAK

GOT THIS OFF A WARLOCK I KILLED DOWN BY LEEDS WAY.

YOU WOULDN'T BELIEVE THE FIGHT HE PUT UP—

GOD DAMN THAT DEVIL STARKWEATHER FOR SHOWING YOU WHAT HE DID...

...BUT YOU MUST KNOW IT'S NOT LIKE THAT ANYMORE.

THE ACCORDS HAVE FORBIDDEN SPOILS. IT WAS JUST A DREAM.

BUT NO.

THIS IS THE DREAM.

CAN YOU SLEEP NOW? WE'RE MEANT TO RISE EARLY TOMORROW.

STARKWEATHER IS LENDING US HIS CARRIAGE SO THAT WE MIGHT INVESTIGATE RAVENSCAR MANOR.

YOU, OF COURSE, ARE WELCOME TO REMAIN HERE. YOU NEED NOT ACCOMPANY US.

STAY HERE WITHOUT YOU? I WOULD PREFER NOT TO.

57

SWISH

NO.

NO, I DON'T KNOW THAT, WILL.

YOU HAVE MADE IT VERY CLEAR WHAT KIND OF USE YOU HAVE FOR ME. YOU THINK I AM A TOY FOR YOUR AMUSEMENTS.

CAN YOU TELL ME YOU DID NOT MEAN WHAT YOU SAID THAT NIGHT ON THE ROOF?

......

NO.

NO, THE ANGEL FORGIVE ME, I CAN'T SAY THAT.

PLEASE GO AWAY, WILL.

TESSA—

PLEASE.

TESSA, HOW ARE YOU FEELING?

I JUST HAVE A HEADACHE.

I'VE TOLD GOTTSHALL TO DROP YOU STRAIGHT AT THE STATION ON YOUR RETURN, NO NEED FOR LINGERING. I TRUST YOU'VE GOTTEN EVERYTHING YOU NEED.

YES, SIR. YOU'VE BEEN VERY GRACIOUS.

SWISH

STAB

I...am...a...
warning...
from the
Magister.

A warning...
to you, Will
Herondale...
and to all
Nephilim...

The Magister
says...you must
cease your
investigation. The
past...is the past.
Leave Mortmain's
buried, or your
family will pay
the price.

HOW DID
MORTMAIN
BRING MY FAMILY
HERE? DID HE
THREATEN
THEM? WHAT
HAS HE DONE?

I...
am...a...
warning...
from...

STAB

CLATTER

SLASH

SLASH

WHAM

WILL.

WILL, ENOUGH.

LOOK. WE MUST GO.

IF WE WANT TO DRAW THEM OFF, AWAY FROM YOUR FAMILY, WE MUST LEAVE.

WILL, YOU KNOW YOU CANNOT GO NEAR THEM.

IF NOTHING ELSE, IT IS THE LAW. IF WE BRING DANGER TO THEM, THE CLAVE WILL NOT MOVE TO HELP THEM IN ANY WAY.

THEY ARE NOT SHADOWHUNTERS ANYMORE.

THE INFERNAL DEVICES
CLOCKWORK PRINCE

CHAPTER 11

LOSE HER?

...I DO LOVE HER, BUT IT'S NOT JUST ABOUT HER.

THIS IS ABOUT TESSA. I KNEW IT WAS.

IS THIS CURSE SUPPOSED TO BE SOME BUSINESS ABOUT TAKING AWAY YOUR ABILITY TO LOVE?

BECAUSE THAT'S NONSENSE. I'VE SEEN YOU WITH YOUR PARABATAI, JEM. YOU LOVE HIM, DON'T YOU?

JEM IS MY GREAT SIN. DON'T TALK TO ME ABOUT JEM.

DON'T TALK TO YOU ABOUT JEM, DON'T TALK TO YOU ABOUT TESSA.

YOU WANT ME TO OPEN A PORTAL TO THE DEMON WORLDS FOR YOU, AND YOU WON'T TALK TO ME OR TELL ME WHY? I WON'T DO IT, WILL.

......

I SAW MY FAMILY, MY YOUNGER SISTER, TODAY. I NEVER THOUGHT I WOULD SEE THEM AGAIN. THEY CANNOT BE NEAR ME.

WHY? WHAT DID THEY DO THAT WAS SO TERRIBLE?

WHAT DID THEY DO? NOTHING. IT IS ME. I AM POISON.

POISON TO THEM. POISON TO ANYONE WHO LOVES ME.

WILL?

...I WAS TWELVE, LIVING WITH MY PARENTS IN WALES.

IT WAS A RAINY DAY. I WAS BORED, GOING THROUGH MY FATHER'S OLD THINGS FROM HIS LIFE AS A SHADOWHUNTER.

I FOUND A SMALL ENGRAVED BOX IN A FALSE DRAWER OF HIS DESK. OF COURSE THE FIRST THING I DID WAS OPEN IT.

FWOOOSH

I KNEW THEN THAT I HAD TO GET AWAY FROM ALL MY FAMILY BEFORE I BROUGHT THE SAME HORROR DOWN UPON THEM.

I LEFT THAT NIGHT, FOLLOWING THE ROADS TO LONDON.

SINCE THAT DAY I HAVE STRIVEN TO MAKE SURE NO ONE GETS NEAR ME, BEING CRUEL TO THOSE I HAVE CHOSEN TO MAKE MY HOME WITH.

TESSA...I HAVE BEEN FOUL ENOUGH TO HER, BUT THERE WAS A TIME I THOUGHT HER DEAD...

...AND I SHOWED HER—I LET HER SEE WHAT I FELT.

AND JEM...?

HE'S DYING ANYWAY.

BUT I CRUSHED HER, AS BRUTALLY AS I COULD. I IMAGINE SHE SIMPLY HATES ME NOW.

JEM IS WHAT I HAVE ALLOWED MYSELF. I TELL MYSELF, IF HE DIES, IT IS NOT MY FAULT.

NO ONE CAN LIVE WITH NOTHING.

JEM IS ALL I HAVE.

...YOU HAVE NEVER TOLD ANYONE OF THIS CURSE?

I COULD NOT.

HOW COULD I BE SURE THEY WOULD FORM NO ATTACHMENT TO ME, ONCE THEY KNEW THE TRUTH?

A STORY LIKE THIS MIGHT ENGENDER PITY, PITY COULD BECOME ATTACHMENT AND THEN.

AND THEN THEY WOULD DIE.

I STILL WON'T HELP YOU.

!

DROPPING YOU INTO THE DEMON REALMS IS LIKE DROPPING A RAT INTO A PIT FULL OF TERRIERS.

YOU THINK YOU'RE THE ONLY PERSON WHO'S EVER LOST ANYONE?

THIS IS MADNESS, YOU KNOW. GO HOME. SLEEP IT OFF.

DON'T MAKE IT SOUND LIKE SOME ORDINARY SORT OF GRIEF. THEY SAY TIME HEALS ALL WOUNDS...

...BUT THAT PRESUMES THE SOURCE OF THE GRIEF IS FINITE. OVER. THIS IS A FRESH WOUND EVERY DAY.

YOU WOULD BE DOING ME A MERCY, SENDING ME TO THE DEMON REALMS. IT IS MY ONLY CHANCE.

YOU ARE IN LOVE AND YOU THINK THAT IS ALL THERE IS IN THE WORLD. BUT THE WORLD IS BIGGER THAN YOU, WILL, AND YOUR LIFE IS NOT YOURS TO THROW AWAY.

IF THAT IS ALL YOU HAVE TO SAY TO ME, THEN SO HAVE YOU— WARLOCK.

THEN NOTHING IS MINE.

SWISH

81

WILL'S GONE, AFTER SEEING HIS SISTER?

RAVENSCAR MANOR...OF ALL THE PLACES I THOUGHT THEY'D GO...

SLAM

WHAT DO YOU MEAN, OF ALL THE PLACES YOU THOUGHT THEY'D GO?

DID YOU KNOW THAT WILL'S FAMILY HAD MOVED?

......

AFTER WILL'S PARENTS CAME HERE TO SEE HIM, WHEN HE WAS TWELVE, AND HE SENT THEM AWAY...WILL MADE A REQUEST.

HE CAN'T HAVE CARED ABOUT HIS FAMILY THAT MUCH IN THE FIRST PLACE OR HE WOULDN'T HAVE LEFT THEM.

HOW CAN YOU SAY THAT? YOU DON'T KNOW WHY HE LEFT.

PLEASE PROMISE ME YOU'LL TELL ME IF THEY DIE, CHARLOTTE.

IT WAS SUCH AN ODD REQUEST FOR A LITTLE BOY TO MAKE. I—I HAD TO SAY YES.

SO I HIRED RAGNOR FELL TO LOOK INTO WILL'S FAMILY FOR THE NEXT THREE YEARS.

THE FOURTH YEAR HE CAME BACK AND TOLD ME THAT THE HERONDALES HAD MOVED AFTER WILL'S FATHER LOST THEIR HOUSE GAMBLING.

FELL COULD FIND NO FURTHER TRACE OF THEM...AND NOW THEY'RE LIVING IN A HOUSE THAT USED TO BELONG TO MORTMAIN?

THIS IS NOT WHERE I THOUGHT THIS ROAD WOULD LEAD. WE SOUGHT MORTMAIN AND WE FOUND WILL'S FAMILY. HE ENCIRCLES US, LIKE THAT CURSED OUROBOROS THAT IS HIS SYMBOL.

CAN YOU HAVE RAGNOR FELL LOOK INTO WILL'S FAMILY'S WELFARE AGAIN?

YES, YES, OF COURSE. I WILL WRITE TO HIM IMMEDIATELY.

TESSA...I HATE TO ASK THIS OF YOU, BUT WE MUST LEAVE NO STONE UNTURNED.

DO YOU STILL HAVE THE BUTTON FROM STARKWEATHER'S COAT?

OF COURSE. BUT LET ME BE LEFT ALONE WHILE I TRY.

I DO NOT WANT TO ACQUAINT MYSELF WITH HIM...

ROLL
ROL

WOBBLE

HAAH.

HAAH.

!!!

I'D BETTER REIN IN MY DAY-DREAMING...

...OR I'LL END UP AS MAD AS OLD STARK-WEATHER.

I TOLD CHARLOTTE ABOUT STARKWEATHER'S MEMORIES OF THE SHADE FAMILY, BUT SHE LOOKED DISAPPOINTED WHEN I SAID I HAD DISCOVERED NOTHING ABOUT RAVENSCAR MANOR.

THANK YOU SO MUCH FOR YOUR HELP, TESSA.

MAIL FOR ME? THANK YOU SOPHIE.

A LETTER FOR YOU, MISS.

Dear sensible Miss Gray, I write to you on behalf of a mutual friend, one William Herondale.

WAIT FOR ME IN YOUR ROOM. I WILL GET DRESSED AND BE THERE MOMENTARILY.

THIS IS WILL'S ROOM.

GRACIOUS. I'VE NEVER BEEN IN HERE.

I WAS STARTING TO IMAGINE HE SLEPT UPSIDE DOWN, LIKE A BAT.

HA-HA...

WAIT HERE. I NEED TO FIND SOMETHING.

DROP
DROP

THE LETTERS I WROTE TO NATE FROM THE DARK HOUSE?!

WHAT ARE THEY DOIN' HERE?

TESSA, I FOUND IT.

IT'S A DAGGER HIS FATHER GAVE HIM. IT SHOULD HAVE A STRONG ENOUGH IMPRINT OF WILL FOR US TO TRACK HIM WITH IT.

CLIP CLOP CLIP CLOP CLIP CLOP CLIP CLOP

BRICK LANE, NEAR WHITECHAPEL HIGH STREET.

IT'S A CRUEL PART OF THE CITY WE'RE GOING INTO. THE EAST END. THE SLUMS.

I WANT YOU TO BE CAREFUL, AND TO STAY CLOSE BY ME.

DO YOU KNOW WHAT WILL'S DOING THERE?

I DON'T. I ONLY GOT A SENSE—A FLEETING IMAGE OF THE STREET—FROM THE TRACKING SPELL.

THE REASON WHY YOU CAN SENSE HIM...IS BECAUSE YOU'RE PARABATAI. HOW DID THAT HAPPEN?

HE ASKED ME, OR RATHER TOLD ME, WHILE WE WERE TRAINING WITH LONGSWORDS.

I SAID NO, BUT HE BET ME HE COULD GET MY SWORD AWAY FROM ME, AND HE SUCCEEDED.

WHY DIDN'T YOU WANT TO DO IT WHEN HE FIRST ASKED YOU?

HE MUST HAVE BEEN TRAINING WITHOUT MY KNOWING ABOUT IT, BECAUSE I'D NEVER HAVE AGREED IF I'D THOUGHT HE WAS THAT GOOD WITH A LONGSWORD.

YOU CAN CHOOSE ONLY ONE PARABATAI IN YOUR LIFE. YOU CAN'T HAVE A SECOND, EVEN IF THE FIRST ONE DIES.

BAM BAM
BAM

FMP

NO. NO NEPHILIM.

WE'RE NOT HERE FOR THE CLAVE. IT'S PERSONAL. WE'RE LOOKING FOR A FRIEND. TAKE US TO HIM, AND WE WON'T BOTHER YOU FURTHER.

I KNOW WHO YOU'RE LOOKING FOR. THERE'S ONLY ONE OF YOUR KIND HERE.

THIS IS WHERE WILL COMES TO BUY THE— TO BUY WHAT I NEED.

ALTHOUGH WHY HE WOULD BE HERE NOW...

MADRAN SAYS WE HAVE WHAT YOU WANT, SILVER BOY.

NO NEED FOR PRETENSE.

I TOLD YOU, WE'RE HERE FOR A FRIEND.

THERE IS LITTLE OF THE *YIN FEN* LEFT, AND WHEN IT IS GONE, YOU WILL DIE. WE STRUGGLE TO OBTAIN MORE, BUT LATELY THE DEMAND—

SPARE US YOUR ATTEMPTS TO SELL YOUR MERCHANDISE. WHERE IS OUR FRIEND?

...THERE.

IF YOU DO NOT HELP ME, I WILL CHANGE INTO YOU, AND I WILL LIFT HIM MYSELF. AND THEN EVERYONE WILL SEE WHAT YOU LOOK LIKE IN A DRESS.

DO YOU UNDERSTAND?

HELP ME WITH HIM.

LET ME GO—

TELL ME THIS IS NOT A DREAM.

LISTEN, CARSTAIRS, YOU HAVEN'T ANY OF THE NEEDFUL ON YOU, HAVE YOU?

I'D STUMP UP, BUT I'M FLAT OUT.

NOW WE'RE ALL THREE TOGETHER.

SHUT UP.

WHAT DID HE SAY?

HE WANTS ME TO PAY FOR HIS DRUGS.

LET ME GO. I CAN STAND.

SLAP

YOU DID NOT HAVE TO COME AND FETCH ME LIKE SOME CHILD.

I WAS HAVING QUITE A PLEASANT TIME.

GOD DAMN YOU.

GET HIM INTO THE CARRIAGE.

CLIP CLOP

CLIP CLOP

CLIP CLOP

CLIP CLOP

WE'RE HERE.

SWISH

CYRIL, HELP WILL TO HIS ROOM.

JEM...

JEM?

JEM! JEM, STOP! YOUR VIOLIN— YOUR LOVELY VIOLIN— YOU'LL RUIN IT.

WHAT DOES IT MATTER? I'M DYING. I WON'T OUTLAST THE DECADE. WHAT DOES IT MATTER IF THE VIOLIN GOES BEFORE I DO?

......!

I WILL DIE, AND YOU KNOW IT, TESS. PROBABLY WITHIN THE NEXT YEAR. I AM DYING, AND I HAVE NO FAMILY IN THE WORLD...

I DON'T THINK THAT'S WHAT WILL MEANT TO DO AT ALL.

...AND THE ONE PERSON I TRUSTED MORE THAN ANY OTHER MADE SPORT OF WHAT IS KILLING ME.

HE KNOWS WHAT IT MEANS TO ME.

YOU'RE BURNING UP. YOU SHOULD BE RESTING—

LIKE WHAT?

DO YOU THINK I DO NOT KNOW THAT WHEN YOU TAKE MY HAND, IT IS ONLY SO THAT YOU CAN FEEL MY PULSE?

DO YOU THINK I DO NOT KNOW THAT WHEN YOU LOOK INTO MY EYES, IT IS ONLY TO SEE HOW MUCH OF THE DRUG I HAVE TAKEN?

DON'T TOUCH ME LIKE THAT.

AS IF YOU WERE A NURSE AND I WERE YOUR PATIENT.

IF I WERE ANOTHER MAN A NORMAL MAN, I MIGHT HAVE HOPES, PRESUMPTION EVEN. I MIGHT—

NI HEN PIAO LIANG...

WHAT DOES IT MEAN?

IT MEANS THAT YOU ARE BEAUTIFUL.

I DID NOT WANT TO TELL YOU BEFORE. I DID NOT WANT YOU TO THINK I WAS TAKING LIBERTIES.

THE INFERNAL DEVICES
CLOCKWORK PRINCE

CHAPTER 12

I COULDN'T
SLEEP AT ALL...
WHY IS IT THEY
ALL TELL ME TO
GET OUT AFTER
I KISS THEM?

I SUPPOSE YOU ALL KNOW BY NOW THAT I WENT TO AN OPIUM DEN LAST NIGHT.

WHERE'S JEM...?

EGG♥

......

DID YOU HEAR ME? I SAID I WENT TO AN OPIUM DEN LAST NIGHT.

ARE YOU QUITE A HOPELESS ADDICT NOW?

I HOPE IT WASN'T ONE OF THOSE PLACES THAT'S RUN BY IFRITS.

IT'S EXACTLY ONE OF THOSE PLACES.

HOW DO YOU KNOW?

I USED A TRACKING SPELL TO FIND WILL LAST NIGHT. I WAS GROWING CONCERNED.

YOU WORRY TOO MUCH. IT'S SILLY.

JEM!!

YOU'RE QUITE RIGHT. I WON'T MAKE THAT MISTAKE AGAIN.

SOME OF THEM HAD ALREADY BEGUN TO CHANGE COLOR. QUITE A FEW HAD SILVER HAIR OR EYES. IF YOU CAN GET AHOLD OF WOOLSEY SCOTT, I'D SPEAK TO HIM AS SOON AS POSSIBLE.

I HEARD ONE OF THE WEREWOLVES SAY THAT *YIN FEN* WORKS AS A STIMULANT, AND THAT IT PLEASED THE MAGISTER THAT THE DRUG KEPT THEM WORKING ALL NIGHT LONG.

DEAR GOD, I HOPE SCOTT ISN'T CAUGHT UP WITH THE MAGISTER.

DE QUINCEY FIRST, NOW THE WOLVES— ALL OUR ALLIES.

PERHAPS YOU SHOULD BE THERE WHEN I SPEAK WITH SCOTT, HENRY. YOU ARE THE HEAD OF THE INSTITUTE—

OH, NO. DARLING, YOU'LL BE QUITE ALL RIGHT WITHOUT ME.

YOU'RE SUCH A GENIUS WIT THESE NEGO TIATIONS, A I'M SIMPLY NOT.

AND BESIDES, THE INVENTION I'M WORKING ON NOW COULD SHATTER THE WHOLE CLOCKWORK ARMY INTO PIECES, IF I GET THE FORMULATIONS RIGHT!

CHARLOTTE...?

SLIDE

SLAM

WHAT IS IT? WHAT HAVE I DONE WRONG?

......

WHY IS HE HERE?

HEY THERE. I KNOW IT'LL DRIVE YOU MAD IF I WATCH THE TRAINING, AND I COULD DO WITH A LITTLE MADNESS THIS MORNING.

GRRRRR

GABRIEL, WE'RE MEANT TO BE WORKING, NOT SNAPPING AT OTHERS OVER YEARS-OLD PETTY DISAGREEMENTS.

HMPH! WHEN WE RUN THE INSTITUTE, THIS TRAINING ROOM WILL BE FAR BETTER KEPT UP AND SUPPLIED.

CHARLOTTE RUNS THIS INSTITUTE.

NOT FOR LONG. MY FATHER WILL TAKE IT FROM HER.

GRANVILLE FAIRCHILD WANTED THE INSTITUTE TO GO TO HIS DAUGHTER, AND THE CONSUL MADE IT HAPPEN.

EVERYONE KNOWS IT. EVERYONE KNOWS HE DOESN'T REALLY LOVE HER. HOW COULD HE—

!!

BUT EVEN THOUGH FAIRCHILD IS DEAD, WE CAN STILL TAKE THAT AWAY FROM HIM. HE WAS HATED—SO HATED THAT NO ONE WOULD HAVE MARRIED CHARLOTTE IF HE HADN'T PAID OFF THE BRANWELLS TO HAND HENRY OVER.

SLAP

SOPHIE!

...MY MOTHER'S DYING WISH WAS THAT WE WOULD TAKE THE INSTITUTE FROM THE FAIRCHILDS.

AND I WILL MAKE IT COME TRUE.

SLAM

THERE GOES GABRIEL'S CARRIAGE.

THAT WAS FAST.

FWUMP

WILL.

ABOUT WHAT HAPPENED LAST NIGHT...

?

THAT HE HIT YOU ONLY SHOWS HOW CAPABLE YOU ARE OF DRIVING EVEN SAINTS TO MADNESS.

I MUST CONFESS, I REMEMBER VERY LITTLE (LAST NIGHT.

YOU SHOULD THINK ABOUT THE WAY THE THINGS YOU DO AFFECT JEM.

JEM HIT ME?!

WELL, JEM HIT YOU. AND YOU DESERVED IT.

COME ALONG NOW, EVERYONE, SIT DOWN. THERE'S NO NEED TO BE INTIMIDATED BY ME.

CHARLOTTE, RING FOR SOME TEA. I'M PARCHED.

OH! GUNPOWDER TEA! FROM CEYLON, I PRESUME? HAVE YOU EVER HAD THE TEA IN MARRAKECH? THEY DRENCH IT IN SUGAR OR HONEY—

MR. SCOTT, WE REALLY MUST DISCUSS THE SITUATION AT HAND.

NO SERIOUS DISCUSSION, PLEASE, UNTIL I'VE HAD MY TEA AND A SMOKE.

SMILE

YOU'RE CONCERNED THAT I'M BETRAYING YOU THE WAY YOU THOUGHT DE QUINCEY DID, THAT I'M IN LEAGUE WITH THE MAGISTER.

I HAD THOUGHT...

...THAT PERHAPS LONDON'S DOWNWORLDERS FELT BETRAYED BY THE INSTITUTE AFTER WHAT HAPPENED WITH DE QUINCEY. HIS DEATH—

I DESPISED DE QUINCEY. THE WEREWOLF HE KILLED FOR HIS ATTACHMENT TO CAMILLE BELCOURT

YOU'VE TAKEN CARE OF DE QUINCEY FOR ME. YOU'VE NO IDEA HOW GRATEFUL I AM.

FOR THIS, YOU HAVE EARNED A FAVOR. I WILL TELL YOU WHAT I KNOW, THOUGH IT ISN'T MUCH.

MORTMAIN CAME TO ME IN THE EARLY DAYS, WANTING ME TO JOIN WITH HIM IN THE PANDEMONIUM CLUB.

I REFUSED, FOR DE QUINCEY HAD ALREADY JOINED, AND I WOULD NOT BE PART OF A CLUB THAT HAD HIM IN IT.

THE ULTIMATE PURPOSE OF THE CLUB IS THE DESTRUCTION OF ALL SHADOWHUNTERS.

NEWS HAS REACHED ME OF A GROUP OF YOUNG WOLVES, UNSWORN TO ANY PACK, WHO HAVE BEEN DOING SOME SORT OF UNDERGROUND WORK AND HAVE BEEN GETTING PAID VERY WELL FOR IT. I DID NOT KNOW ABOUT THE DRUG.

IT WILL KEEP THOSE WOLVES WORKING FOR HIM...

...UNTIL THEY DROP FROM EXHAUSTION OR THE DRUG KILLS THEM.

THIS *YIN FEN*, THIS SILVER POWDER, IT IS WHAT YOUR FRIEND JAMES CARSTAIRS IS ADDICTED TO, ISN'T IT? AND HE'S ALIVE.

JEM SURVIVES IT BECAUSE HE USES AS LITTLE AS POSSIBLE, AS INFREQUENTLY AS POSSIBLE AND EVEN THEN, IT WILL KILL HIM IN THE END. AS WOULD WITHDRAWING FROM IT.

WELL, WELL. I DO HOPE THAT THE MAGISTER MERRILY BUYING THE STUFF UP DOESN'T CREATE A SHORTAGE, IN THAT CASE.

!!

WILL?!

HOW DID I NOT THINK OF THIS!

WILL?

JAMES!

I NEED TO TALK TO YOU. LET ME INTO YOUR ROOM.

......

HOW MUCH YIN FEN DO YOU HAVE?

?

I HAVE ENOUGH OF IT FOR AT LEAST ANOTHER MONTH.

WE WILL BE IN HIS POWER.

MORTMAIN'S MINIONS HAVE BEEN BUYING UP THE *YIN FEN* SUPPLY IN THE EAST END. IF YOU RUN OUT AND HE IS THE ONLY ONE WITH A SUPPLY...

UNLESS YOU WERE WILLING TO LET ME DIE, OF COURSE, WHICH WOULD BE THE SENSIBLE COURSE OF ACTION.

I WOULD *NOT* BE WILLING.

I HAD BEGUN TO WONDER IF YOU WERE CAPABLE OF THE DESIRE TO SPARE ANYONE SUFFERING.

I...I SPOKE TO TESSA TODAY. I WENT TO THAT DEN BECAUSE I COULD NOT STOP THINKING ABOUT MY FAMILY, AND I WANTED—I NEEDED—TO STOP THINKING.

YOU HURT EVERYONE, WILL.

NOT YOU! I NEVER MEANT TO HURT YOU. YOU HAVE TO FORGIVE ME. OR I'D BE—

IT DID NOT CROSS MY MIND THAT IT WOULD LOOK TO YOU AS IF I WERE MAKING A MOCKERY OUT OF YOUR SICKNESS. I DO HOPE THAT YOU WILL FORGIVE ME.

ALONE?

AND WHOSE FAULT IS THAT?

BUT NOW... SOMETHING HAS CHANGED.

SOPHIE? WHAT ARE YOU DOING AT THIS HOUR?

!!

ERM...

IT'S...IT'S MISS JESSAMINE. SHE...SHE'S BEEN SLIPPING AWAY IN THE NIGHTS.

heart is bursting u tomorrow nig however great t es for nothing an ear the white dre I like it o pearls, as the gen is always. N.G.

AND TONIGHT, I FOUND THIS.

BENEDICT LIGHTWOOD presents his compliments to MISS JESSAMINE LOVELACE and requests the honor of her company at a masquerade ball given on Tuesday next, the 27th of July. RSVP.

IT'S AN INVITATION FROM NATE, TO A LIGHTWOOD BALL?!

THE WALL IS COMING DOWN.

WHERE IS JESSAMINE? I MUST SPEAK TO HER THIS INSTANT.

SEE, THAT'S THE THING...

I-I HIT HER ON THE HEAD WITH A MIRROR. SHE...SHE FOUND ME WITH THE INVITATION IN MY HAND. I TRIED TO HIDE IT, BUT SHE'D ALREADY SEEN IT. SHE HAD SUCH A MENACING LOOK ON HER FACE WHEN SHE CAME REACHING FOR IT, I COULDN'T HELP MYSELF.

YOU DID THIS, SOPHIE?!

EEEK!

STOP IT. YOU'RE FRIGHTENING THE POOR GIRL MORE THAN SHE'S ALREADY FRIGHTENED.

SOPHIE, MY DEAR, MANY'S THE TIME I HA' WANTED TO HI' HER MYSELF. NO ONE COULI' BLAME YOU.

I THINK I MAY BE IN LOVE WITH YOU. MARRIAGE COULD BE ON THE CARDS.

AN IRATZE.

THAT IS, A HEALING RUNE, AND A "SLEEP NOW" RUNE. THIS SHOULD KEEP HER QUIET, AT LEAST UNTIL MORNING.

EVEN THOUGH YOU ARE THE PERFECT PICTURE OF JESSAMINE, I CAN SEE TESSA THROUGH IT SOMEHOW.

IT'S FASCINATING.

AS IF, IF I WERE TO SCRAPE AWAY A LAYER OF PAINT, THERE WOULD BE MY TESSA UNDERNEATH.

I ROLLED MY EYES WHEN HE SAID I SHOULD BE READY TO SWOON AT HIS FINERY, BUT...HE IS REALLY BEAUTIFUL.

I AM NOT JESSAMINE, BUT I AM NOT *YOUR* TESSA EITHER.

I AM AFRAID THAT I MIGHT MAKE A MISTAKE IN FRONT OF NATE.

CLIP CLOP CLIP CLOP

YOU ARE A GOOD ACTRESS, AND YOU KNOW YOUR BROTHER.

AND IN THE EVENT THAT SOMETHING GOES AWRY, I WILL BE THERE.

EVEN IF YOU DON'T SEE ME, TESS, I'LL BE THERE. REMEMBER THAT.

IF WARLOCKS ARE MADE BY HAVING ONE DEMON PARENT AND ONE HUMAN PARENT, WHAT HAPPENS IF ONE OF THOSE PARENTS IS A SHADOWHUNTER?

...WILL, I HAVE A QUESTION...

THE CHILD WOULD BE BORN DEAD. THEY ALWAYS ARE.

WHY DO YOU WANT TO KNOW THESE THINGS?

I WANT TO KNOW WHAT I AM. I BELIEVE I AM SOME... COMBINATION THAT HAS NOT BEEN SEEN BEFORE.

HAVE YOU EVER THOUGHT OF TRANSFORMING YOURSELF INTO ONE OF YOUR PARENTS?

PERHAPS YOU ARE A CLOCKWORK GIRL.

I HAVE THOUGHT OF IT. OF COURSE I HAVE. BUT I HAVE NOTHING OF THEM LEFT, EXCEPT THE ANGEL NECKLACE, WHICH HAS BEEN MINE FOR SO LONG THAT IT DOESN'T WORK.

PERHAPS MORTMAIN'S WARLOCK FATHER BUILT YOU, AND NOW MORTMAIN SEEKS THE SECRET OF HOW TO CREATE SUCH A PERFECT FACSIMILE OF LIFE WHEN ALL HE CAN BUILD ARE HIDEOUS MONSTROSITIES.

START

GRAB

NATE!

WHAT IS IT, JESS? YOU LOOK AS IF YOU'VE SEEN A GHOST.

I—A SUDDEN FEAR CAME OVER ME, THAT YOU WOULD NOT BE HERE.

I THOUGHT YOU'D NEVER GET HERE, JESSIE DEAR.

BENEDICT, UP TO HIS OLD TRICKS. RATHER DISGUSTING.

THAT'S A DEMON, ISN'T IT?

OF COURSE IT IS, SILLY BUNNY. THAT'S WHAT BENEDICT FANCIES. DEMON WOMEN.

AH, JESSIE, DID YOU TAKE CARE OF THAT LITTLE THING I ASKED YOU TO DO?

??

I ASK MYSELF OFTEN WHY MORTMAIN FAVORS HIM SO AND WISHES TO SEE HIM INSTALLED IN THE INSTITUTE SO BADLY.

WELL, THE MAGISTER CONTROLS BENEDICT AS IF HE WERE A PUPPET, SO I GUESS HE COULD USE HIM TO DESTROY THE COUNCIL FROM WITHIN, WHILE THE AUTOMATON ARMY DESTROYS THEM FROM WITHOUT.

TO HIDE *THE BOOK OF THE WHITE* IN MY SISTER'S ROOM?

I HAVE WANTED TO DO THIS EVERY MOMENT OF EVERY HOUR OF EVERY DAY THAT I HAVE BEEN WITH YOU SINCE THE DAY I MET YOU.

HE'S BEING SO GENTLE...

I WANT HIM CLOSER... IT'S LIKE AN ACHE...

THE INFERNAL DEVICES
CLOCKWORK PRINCE

JESSAMINE, ARE YOU AWAKE...?

I'D LIKE TO ASK YOU SOME QUESTIONS ABOUT THIS INVITATION.

?!

AND THERE IS LITTLE ADVANTAGE IN FALSEHOOD NOW, SINCE TESSA ALREADY WENT TO THE PARTY AND SPOKE WITH HER BROTHER THERE.

YOU WENT AS ME?! DISGUSTING CREATURE!! WHAT DID YOU DO TO NATE?!

MY BROTHER IS A LYING MURDERER, AND HE DOES NOT LOVE YOU.

HE WILL ABANDON YOU, IF HE DOES NOT KILL YOU FIRST.

JESSA-MINE!

BUT I...!!

HOW LONG HAVE YOU BEEN MEETING HIM IN SECRET?

HE SENT ME A MESSAGE ONLY A FEW DAYS AFTER MORTMAIN INVADED THE INSTITUTE.

HE APOLOGIZED FOR HIS BEHAVIOR TOWARD ME, AND SAID THAT HE HAD NOT BEEN ABLE TO FORGET MY GRACIOUSNESS OR MY BEAUTY.

FLINCH FLINCH

I WANTED TO IGNORE HIM, BUT THE LETTERS KEPT COMING...AND HE PROPOSED THE SECOND TIME WE MET.

HE SAID THAT HE WAS ONLY WORKING FOR MORTMAIN UNTIL HE COULD PUT TOGETHER ENOUGH OF A FORTUNE TO LIVE COMFORTABLY. HE SAID HE WOULD NOT LIVE OFF HIS WIFE. IS THAT NOT NOBLE?

WHAT DID YOU TELL NATHANIEL?

EVERYTHING.

I WARNED HIM ABOUT THE TRIP TO YORK. THAT IS WHY HE SENT THE AUTOMATONS TO WILL'S FAMILY'S HOME.

148

WHY HAS BENEDICT AGREED TO WORK HAND IN GLOVE WITH MORTMAIN?

LOOSE FLOORBOARD... NEAR THE FIREPLACE...

MORTMAIN IS HOLDING SOMETHING OVER HIM, SOMETHING HE WANTS.

I DON'T KNOW WHAT IT IS. BUT HE WILL DO ANYTHING TO GET IT.

HOW CLOSE IS MORTMAIN TO REALIZING HIS PLAN?

HAS HE MANAGED TO OPEN THE PYXIS?

I...I DON'T KNOW.

I DON'T THINK SO...

SO YOU TOLD NATE EVERYTHING, AND HE TOLD YOU NOTHING.

HE WOULD HAVE KNOWN SHE MIGHT HAVE BEEN CAUGHT, AND HE WOULD HAVE THOUGHT SHE'D CRACK UNDER TORTURE AND SPILL EVERYTHING.

HE HATES YOU, YOU KNOW.

HE SAYS THAT ALL HIS LIFE YOU LOOKED DOWN ON HIM.

I KNOW. AND I DON'T CARE.

THEN DID YOU KNOW THIS?

THAT YOUR FATHER WAS A DEMON, AND YOUR MOTHER WAS A SHADOW-HUNTER?

...THAT'S NOT POSSIBLE. WILL TOLD ME THAT THE OFFSPRING OF SHADOWHUNTERS AND DEMONS ARE STILLBORN.

NO. NO, IT ISN'T POSSIBLE.

BUT SHE'S TELLING THE TRUTH AS SHE BELIEVES IT.

YOU SENT NO MESSAGE. ALTHOUGH THAT DOESN'T MEAN I DIDN'T KEEP TRACK OF YOU.

ALL DONE WITH YOUR RUSSIAN LOVER?

AND THAT MADE YOU JEALOUS?

CAMILLE.

DID YOU WANT ME TO BE?

HE IS DEAD. SO HE HARDLY REPRESENTS COMPETITION FOR YOU.

YOU MUST LET ME HAVE MY LITTLE DIVERSIONS, MAGNUS.

OTHERWISE?

FIDELITY IS A HUMAN CONCEPT, BASED UPON THE IDEA THAT WE ARE HERE BUT FOR A SHORT TIME. YOU CANNOT DEMAND MY FAITHFULNESS FOR ETERNITY.

HOW FOOLISH OF ME. I THOUGHT I COULD.

YOU ARE BEING RIDICULOUS. I WILL NOT BE DICTATED TO, CERTAINLY NOT BY SOME HALF-BREED.

......

YOU ARE DEVOTED TO ME. YOU HAVE SAID SO YOURSELF. YOUR DEVOTION WILL SIMPLY HAVE TO SUFFER MY DIVERSIONS. IF NOT, I SHALL DROP YOU. I CANNOT IMAGINE YOU WANT THAT.

YOU CAN'T BE SERIOUS. A SHADOWHUNTER?

IT DOESN'T MATTER. I HAVE WILL NOW.

WILL. WILLIAM. WAKE UP. WE MUST GO.

UMM...GO WHERE...?

THE LADY OF THE HOUSE HAS RETURNED.

I HAVE A FRIEND I CAN STAY WITH. YOU GO ALONG BACK TO THE INSTITUTE. I'LL GET TO WORK ON YOUR BLASTED DEMON TOOTH AND SEND A MESSAGE TO YOU WHEN I KNOW ANYTHING.

OKAY.

I CAN SEE THAT YOU ALL KNOW ABOUT JESSAMINE NOW?

YES. SHE WAS QUESTIONED WITH THE MORTAL SWORD AND TAKEN TO THE SILENT CITY.

BEST PLACE FOR HER. WHAT'S THE NEXT STEP?

I SAY WE GO TO THE CLAVE AND REPORT BENEDICT.

HE WILL DENY EVERYTHING.

THEN WE SHOULD INVESTIGATE AND PROCEED ON A SURER FOOTING.

AND HOW DO YOU PROPOSE TO INVESTIGATE? THERE IS A LIMIT TO JESSAMINE'S KNOWLEDGE...

JESSAMINE WOULD NEVER AGREE TO DO IT.

WE DO, HOWEVER, HAVE ONE MORE CONNECTION TO THE MAGISTER. SOMEONE WHO IS LIKELY TO KNOW A GREAT DEAL MORE.

NATE. THROUGH JESSAMINE. HE STILL TRUSTS HER.

OF COURSE SHE WOULDN'T. WE WILL BE ASKING TESSA TO REPRISE HER STARRING ROLE AS JESSAMINE.

THAT'S TOO DANGEROUS. FOR TESSA.

THERE IS MORE TO ALL OF THIS FOR ME THAN THERE IS FOR YOU, YOU KNOW.

I CARE ABOUT THE INSTITUTE TOO. BUT NATE IS WORKING WITH MORTMAIN—WHO WANTS TO TRAP ME AND USE ME, WHO MAY KNOW WHAT I AM.

...VERY WELL.

WE WILL NEED JESSAMINE'S HELP NONETHELESS. IT'S LIKELY THEY HAVE SOME SECRET SIGNAL BETWEEN THEM.

WE'D BETTER GET INTO THE CARRIAGE BEFORE IT STARTS TO RAIN.

OH, DEAR GOD. TELL ME WE AREN'T GOING TO ROLL INTO THE RIVER.

SHAAAAAA

HA-HA. THE CARRIAGES OF THE SILENT CITY TRAVEL ONLY ON LAND, AS FAR AS I KNOW.

JEM.

I...YOU MUST KNOW... HOW VERY MUCH YOUR FRIENDSHIP MEANS TO ME. AND—

PLEASE DON'T. EVERY TIME YOU SAY THAT WORD, "FRIENDSHIP," IT GOES INTO ME LIKE A KNIFE.

TO BE FRIENDS IS A BEAUTIFUL THING, TESSA, BUT I HAVE HOPED FOR A LONG TIME NOW THAT WE MIGHT BE MORE THAN FRIENDS.

AND THEN I HAD THOUGHT AFTER THE OTHER NIGHT THAT PERHAPS MY HOPES WERE NOT IN VAIN. BUT NOW—

NOW I HAVE RUINED EVERYTHING. I AM SO SORRY.

YOU SHOULD NOT HAVE TO APOLOGIZE FOR NOT RETURNING MY FEELINGS.

BUT JEM, I WAS APOLOGIZING FOR MY BEHAVIOR THAT OTHER NIGHT. IT WAS FORWARD AND INEXCUSABLE.

WHAT YOU MUST THINK OF ME...

TESSA, YOU CAN'T THINK THAT, CAN YOU? IT IS I WHO HAS BEHAVED INEXCUSABLY.

I HAVE BARELY BEEN ABLE TO LOOK AT YOU SINCE, THINKING HOW MUCH YOU MUST DESPISE ME.

IF I HAD NOT BEEN IN SUCH A DESPERATE STATE, I WOULD HAVE SHOWN MORE RESTRAINT.

THAT SOUNDS ALMOST PRACTICED, JAMES CARSTAIRS. HOW MANY GIRLS HAVE YOU MADE SWOON WITH THAT OBSERVATION?

THERE IS ONLY ONE GIRL I CARE TO MAKE SWOON.

THE QUESTION IS, DOES SHE?

...SHE DOES.

Welcome to the Silent City, Daughter of Lilith.

JESSAMINE.

DID...DID CHARLOTTE SEND YOU TO BRING ME BACK?

NO...BUT WE NEED YOUR HELP.

IN BETRAYING NATE. BUT I DON'T KNOW ANYTHING. I DON'T EVEN KNOW WHY I'M HERE.

YES, YOU DO. YOU KNOW EXACTLY WHY YOU'RE HERE.

BECAUSE I FELL IN LOVE.

...AT LEAST NATE IS HUMAN.

WE MUST ARRIVE FIRST AND HIDE OURSELVES.

NATE WILL RECOGNIZE THE INSTITUTE'S CARRIAGE. JESSAMINE WAS MOST DECIDEDLY GOING ON FOOT. I SHALL WALK.

I SUGGEST CYRIL TAKES US THERE, THEN RETURNS FOR TESSA.

IT IS DANGEROUS WALKING THE STREETS ALONE.

CYRIL SHOULD FOLLOW HER AT A DISCREET DISTANCE.

...ARE WE ONCE AGAIN LEAVING THE INSTITUTE WITHOUT A SHADOWHUNTER TO PROTECT IT?

YOU CALLED ON ME?

GIDEON LIGHTWOOD?!

THERE. SOPHIE SUGGESTED HIM.

SHALL WE GO, THEN, MISS?

AH, I HAVE FORGOTTEN SOMETHING. WAIT HERE FOR ME, CYRIL.

MY CLOCKWORK ANGEL!

SOPHIE AND GIDEON?!

IS EVERYTHING ALL RIGHT, MISS? DID YOU GET WHAT YOU WANTED?

WELL... WE CAN GO NOW, CYRIL.

IT'S EMPTY, BUT THE FLOOR IS CLEAR OF DUST. THERE HAS BEEN ACTIVITY HERE.

THERE ARE MORE OFFICES THAT WAY. CHARLOTTE AND I WILL SEARCH THEM.

WILL, JEM, YOU EXAMINE THE SECOND FLOOR.

THOUGHT I WERE GOING TER LIVE FOREVER—WORK ALL NIGHT, ALL DAY, NEVER GET TIRED.

THEN WE STARTED DYING OFF, ONE BY ONE.

THE DRUG, IT KILLS YA, BUT 'E NEVER SAID.

I CAME BACK HERE TO SEE IF MAYBE THERE WAS STILL ANY OF IT STASHED SOMEWHERE. BUT THERE'S NONE.

HE KNEW IT WOULD KILL YOU. HE DOESN'T DESERVE YOUR SECRECY. TELL US WHAT HE WAS KEEPING YOU WORKING ON ALL NIGHT AND DAY.

PUTTING THOSE THINGS TOGETHER—

THOSE METAL MEN.

THEY DON'T 'ARF GIVE YOU THE WILLIES, BUT THE MONEY WERE GOOD AND THE DRUGS WERE BETTER—

YOU—

'OW MUCH LONGER 'AVE YOU GOT LEFT?

THE INFERNAL DEVICES
CLOCKWORK PRINCE

CHAPTER 14

DASH

GRAB

THUD

AS IF I'D LET YOU GO.

HE IS STRONGER THAN I AM.

MORE RUTHLESS THAN I AM

URK...

BUT THERE IS ONE THING I CAN DO THAT HE CANNOT.

TESSA.

FWOOOSH

GRIN

THROW

WHAT IN THE BLOODY HELL DO YOU POSSIBLY THINK YOU'RE—

YOU!

TESSIE, WHERE'S YOUR ANGEL?

I COULDN'T WEAR IT. I WAS PRETENDING TO BE JESSAMINE.

YOU...MUST WEAR IT.

WEAR IT ALWAYS... YOU SWEAR?

NATE...

I KNOW... I'M GOING TO BURN, TESSIE...

NATE—

WILL...?

HE PROTECTED YOU, BUT THERE WAS NOTHING TO PROTECT HIM. THE METAL FRAGMENTS SHREDDED HIS BACK.

WE NEED TO GET HIM BACK HOME TO THE INFIRMARY.

TESSA...

DRINK THIS. IT WILL CALM YOU.

HOW ARE YOUR INJURIES?

ONCE ALL THE METAL WAS OUT, THEY WERE ABLE TO USE AN IRATZE ON ME. BY TOMORROW THE WOUNDS WILL BE SCARS.

ARE YOU IN PAIN?

NO...

TESS...

WILL...

IT'S ALL RIGHT. IT DOESN'T MATTER WHAT YOU DO. WE'RE DREAMING, YOU KNOW.

TESS...

IF ONLY WILL REALLY WERE LIKE THIS, NOT JUST IN DREAMS...

YOUR FATHER TRAPPED ME FOR TWENTY YEARS IN THAT THING.

SOMETHING ABOUT THIS STORY STRIKES ME AS ODD.

WHAT IS THAT?

A DEMON, UPON BEING LET OUT OF A PYXIS, IS USUALLY AT ITS WEAKEST, HAVING BEEN STARVED FOR SO LONG.

THAT'S WHY YOU CURSED US. CURSED ME. DO YOU REMEMBER?

TOO WEAK TO CAST A CURSE AS SUBTLE AND STRONG AS THE ONE YOU CLAIM TO HAVE CAST ON WILL.

......

JUST TELL THE TRUTH.

DO YOU REALLY WISH TO DISOBEY ME, MARBAS?

DO YOU WISH TO ANGER MY FATHER?

MARBAS, YOU ARE A BLUE-SKINNED BASTARD!

BURN AND DIE!

EEEEEK!

EVERYTHING I'VE DONE, ALL THE LYING, THE ABANDONMENT OF MY FAMILY, THE UNFORGIVABLE THINGS I SAID TO TESSA—A WASTE. A BLOODY WASTE, AND ALL BECAUSE OF A LIE I WAS STUPID ENOUGH TO BELIEVE.

YOU WERE TWELVE YEARS OLD. YOUR SISTER WAS DEAD. MARBAS WAS A CUNNING CREATURE.

RESIGNING FROM THE INSTITUTE? HOW CAN YOU?

BETTER TO RESIGN THAN TO HAVE CONSUL WAYLAND COME IN OVER MY HEAD AND FORCE ME OUT.

DON'T YOU MEAN "US"? SHOULD I HAVE AT LEAST A SAY IN THIS DECISION?

YOU'VE NEVER TAKEN AN INTEREST IN THE RUNNING OF THE INSTITUTE BEFORE. WHY WOULD YOU NOW?

I DID THINK YOU UNDERSTOOD. YOU KNOW I WANT TO CREATE SOMETHING THAT WILL MAKE THE WORLD BETTER. AND THOUGH I KNOW I WILL ALWAYS COME SECOND FOR YOU—

I'M SORRY. SOMETIMES I GET SO CAUGHT UP IN MY IDEAS.

SECOND FOR ME? YOU COME SECOND FOR ME?!

IT'S ALL RIGHT, LOTTIE. I KNEW WHEN YOU AGREED TO MARRY ME IT WAS BECAUSE YOU NEEDED TO BE MARRIED TO RUN THE INSTITUTE...

...THAT NO ONE WOULD ACCEPT A WOMAN ALONE IN THE POSITION OF DIRECTOR—

DO YOU THINK I DON'T KNOW ABOUT THE MONEY YOUR FATHER OWED MY FATHER, OR THAT MY FATHER PROMISED TO FORGIVE THE DEBT IF YOU'D MARRY ME?

HENRY... HOW CAN YOU SAY SUCH TERRIBLE THINGS TO ME?

!!

CHARLOTTE, WHAT ON EARTH ARE YOU TALKING ABOUT? I KNOW NOTHING OF MY FATHER'S OWING YOURS ANYTHING.

I WENT TO YOUR FATHER BECAUSE I LOVED YOU AND ASKED HIM IF HE WOULD DO ME THE HONOR OF ALLOWING ME TO ASK FOR YOUR HAND IN MARRIAGE. THERE WAS NEVER ANY DISCUSSION OF MONEY!

HE IS A GOOD ENOUGH MAN, BETTER THAN HIS FATHER, AND YOU NEED SOME SORT OF A HUSBAND, CHARLOTTE, IF YOU ARE GOING TO DIRECT THE INSTITUTE.

I'VE FORGIVEN HIS FATHER'S DEBTS, SO THAT MATTER IS CLOSED BETWEEN OUR FAMILIES.

OF COURSE, HE NEVER SAID THAT'S WHY HENRY ASKED TO MARRY ME...

!!

I JUST ASSUMED.

YOU HAVEN'T SEEN TESSA, HAVE YOU?

HENRY, CHARLOTTE.

I ALSO WANT TO ASK YOU—WHAT THE HELL IS THIS?!

WILL, HOW ARE YOUR INJURIES?!

CHARLOTTE, YOU CAN'T GIVE UP THE INSTITUTE! THIS IS OUR HOME. OVER ALL THESE YEARS YOU'VE DONE EVERYTHING FOR ME AS IF I WERE YOUR OWN BLOOD, AND I'VE NEVER TOLD YOU I WAS GRATEFUL.

THAT GOES FOR YOU AS WELL, HENRY. BUT I AM GRATEFUL, AND BECAUSE OF IT I SHALL NOT LET YOU MAKE THIS MISTAKE.

WILL, IT IS OVER. WE HAVE ONLY THREE DAYS TO FIND MORTMAIN.

THE TWO-WEEK LIMIT WAS IN ESSENCE SET BY BENEDICT LIGHTWOOD AS A RIDICULOUS TEST.

A TEST THAT, AS IT TURNS OUT, WAS A CHEAT. HE IS WORKING FOR MORTMAIN. IF WE BUT EXPOSE BENEDICT FOR WHAT HE IS—MORTMAIN'S PUPPET—THE INSTITUTE IS YOURS AGAIN, AND THE SEARCH FOR MORTMAIN CAN CONTINUE.

WE CANNOT DO NOTHING. IT IS WORTH AT LEAST A CONVERSATION, DON'T YOU THINK?

!

EXCELLENT. I'LL GO ROUND UP THE OTHERS.

......

WAS THAT WILL? DID HE REALLY SAY "GRATEFUL"?

YOU KNOW WE HAVE NOT FOUND MORTMAIN. IN A FEW DAYS, THE INSTITUTE MAY BE GIVEN TO BENEDICT LIGHTWOOD...

...AND IT WOULD BE THE END OF OUR LITTLE GROUP.

JEM? IS EVERYTHING ALL RIGHT?

I...I WOULD LIKE TO SPEAK TO YOU IN PRIVATE, TESSA.

WILL AND I PERHAPS WOULD GO TO IDRIS, BUT WE COULD NOT BRING YOU WITH US. YOU ARE NOT A SHADOWHUNTER.

...I SEE.

THAT WAS NOT A NO, I SUPPOSE, THOUGH NEITHER WAS IT A YES.

YOU CAN'T— I'M NOT A SHADOWHUNTER. THEY'LL EXPEL YOU FROM THE CLAVE—

YOUR SITUATION IS UNIQUE, SO THEY WILL HAVE TO TAKE YOUR— OUR— INDIVIDUAL CASE INTO CONSIDERATION, AND THAT COULD TAKE MONTHS. IN THE MEANTIME, THEY CANNOT PREVENT OUR ENGAGEMENT.

JEM!

JEM, SUCH A KINDNESS ON YOUR PART IS INDEED INCREDIBLE. IT DOES YOU CREDIT. BUT I CANNOT LET YOU SACRIFICE YOURSELF IN THAT WAY FOR ME.

SACRIFICE? TESSA, I LOVE YOU.

PLEASE, TAKE THIS.

TESSA, I CANNOT EXPLAIN LOVE. BUT I REMEMBER THE FIRST MOMENT I LOOKED AT YOU...

...AND REALIZED THAT SOMEHOW THE REST OF THE WORLD SEEMED TO VANISH WHEN I WAS WITH YOU.

YOU SPEAK OF SACRIFICE, BUT IT IS NOT MY SACRIFICE I OFFER. IT IS YOURS I ASK OF YOU.

THE INFERNAL DEVICES
CLOCKWORK PRINCE

CHAPTER 15

BOTH OF YOU, COME TO THE DRAWING ROOM.

AS YOU PROBABLY KNOW, WE ARE NEAR THE END OF THE TWO-WEEK PERIOD GRANTED TO US BY CONSUL WAYLAND.

WE HAVE NOT DISCOVERED THE WHEREABOUTS OF MORTMAIN. AND AS NATHANIEL GRAY IS DEAD, WE CAN LEARN NOTHING FROM HIM.

WE CAN CERTAINLY REPORT WHAT WE KNOW ABOUT BENEDICT TO THE CLAVE. HAVEN'T WE ENOUGH EVIDENCE? ENOUGH TO EARN HIM A TRIAL BY THE SWORD, AT LEAST.

WHEN WE TRIED THE SWORD ON JESSAMINE, THERE WERE BLOCKS IN HER MIND PUT THERE BY MORTMAIN. IT MIGHT BE THE SAME WITH BENEDICT.

WE WILL LOOK LIKE FOOLS IF THE SWORD CAN GET NOTHING OUT OF HIM.

I'M RESIGNING.

DEMON POX. MR. LIGHTWOOD'S GOT IT, HAS HAD FOR YEARS.

IT'LL KILL HIM IN A RIGHT COUPLE OF MONTHS IF HE DOESN'T GET THE CURE. AND MORTMAIN SAID HE CAN GET IT FOR HIM.

DEMON POX?!

BUT THE ONLY WAY YOU CAN CONTRACT DEMON POX IS BY HAVING IMPROPER RELATIONS WITH A DEMON—

BENEDICT WAS WITH A DEMON WOMAN AT THAT PARTY OF HIS!

RIGHT! THE ONE WHO HAD A SNAKE FOR A TONGUE!

!!

DON'T THE SYMPTOMS OF DEMON POX BEGIN WITH A SHIELD-SHAPED RASH ON ONE'S BACK THAT SPREADS OVER THE BODY, CREATING CRACKS AND FISSURES IN THE SKIN?

I HAD INQUIRED OF THE SILENT BROTHERS ABOUT MRS. LIGHTWOOD'S DEATH, TO SEE IF BENEDICT HAD ALSO LIED THAT SHE HAD DIED OF GRIEF. IN THE REPORT, IT SAID SHE CUT HER OWN WRISTS...

...BUT THAT SHE HAD A SHIELD-SHAPED RASH ON HER LEFT SHOULDER.

THAT *IS* DEMON POX!

BY THE ANGEL... NO WONDER SHE KILLED HERSELF. BECAUSE HER HUSBAND GAVE HER DEMON POX. AND SHE KNEW IT.

AND BENEDICT CONCEALED THE WHOLE THING BY PUTTING THE BLAME ON CHARLOTTE'S FATHER! HOW IS IT THAT HE IS STILL ALIVE, ANYWAY?

MORTMAIN'S BEEN GIVING HIM DRUGS TO SLOW THE PROGRESS OF THE DISEASE ALL THIS TIME.

IT ONLY SLOWS IT, IT DOESN'T STOP IT, AND THAT'S WHY HE'S SO DESPERATE. HE'LL DO ANYTHING MORTMAIN WANTS.

CLENCH

WHAT HE DID IS COMMIT THE KNOWING MURDER OF ANOTHER SHADOWHUNTER.

THAT WOULD CALL DOWN THE WORST OF ALL PUNISHMENTS.

WE WILL CALL ON BENEDICT IMMEDIATELY.

WILL AND TESSA SHALL COME WITH ME. I'LL NEED YOU AS WITNESSES REGARDING THE PARTY.

BOLT

WILL, BUT YOU WILL FOLLOW MY LEAD, AND THERE WILL BE NO TALK OF DEMON POX UNTIL I SAY SO.

BUT-BUT...

HENRY, PLEASE REMAIN WITH JEM AND GUARD THE INSTITUTE.

YOU'RE SURE YOU DON'T WANT ME TO COME WITH YOU?

QUITE SURE, HENRY.

...OKAY, THEN.

I'D BEST FETCH MY HAT AND GLOVES.

TESSA.

TESSA, I NEED TO SPEAK WITH YOU.

NOW? I GATHERED FROM CHARLOTTE THAT SHE WANTED US TO HURRY—

DAMN HURRYING! I WANT TO TALK TO YOU.

WILL, NOT NOW. I BELIEVE I KNOW WHAT IT IS YOU WANT TO SAY, BUT THIS ISN'T THE TIME OR PLACE, IS IT?

BELIEVE ME, I AM AS EAGER FOR THE TALK AS YOU, FOR IT HAS BEEN WEIGHING HEAVILY ON MY MIND—

YOU ARE?
IT HAS?

WELL, YES.
BUT NOT NOW.
MEET ME IN
THE DRAWING
ROOM LATER,
AFTER WE
GO TO THE
LIGHTWOODS'.

SWISH

IT WAS
VERY BRAVE,
WHAT YOU
DID, SOPHIE,
TELLING THE
TRUTH TO
CHARLOTTE.

BUT I
KNOW SHE'S
DISAPPOINTED
IN ME.

SHE'S NOT.
SHE THINKS
YOU'RE
WONDERFUL,
AND SO DO I.

CHAR-LOTTE.

WILL. MISS GRAY.

ALWAYS A PLEASURE.

THANK YOU, BENEDICT, FOR SEEING US ON SUCH SHORT NOTICE.

OF COURSE. YOU DO KNOW THAT THERE'S NOTHING YOU CAN DO THAT'S GOING TO CHANGE THE OUTCOME OF THIS.

WHAT I AM DOING IS IN THE BEST INTERESTS OF THE INSTITUTE AND THE CLAVE. A WOMAN CANNOT RUN THE INSTITUTE.

YOU'LL BE THANKING ME WHEN YOU'RE HOME WITH HENRY RAISING THE NEXT GENERATION OF SHADOW-HUNTERS.

231

I THINK MOST COUNCIL MEMBERS WOULD CHOOSE A WOMAN OVER A DISSOLUTE REPROBATE WHO FRATERNIZES NOT JUST WITH DOWNWORLDERS BUT ALSO WITH DEMONS.

WILL AND TESSA WERE AT YOUR LAST GATHERING. THEY OBSERVED A GREAT DEAL.

THAT DEMON WOMAN YOU WERE LOUNGING WITH— WAS SHE A FRIEND? ONE DOESN'T USUALLY LET ONE'S BUSINESS ASSOCIATES LICK ONE'S FACE.

YOU ARE FOOLISH TO THINK THE COUNCIL WILL BELIEVE ANY OF YOUR LIES. WORDS OF A DOWNWORLDER AND A CERTIFIABLE LUNATIC WHO FRATERNIZES WITH WARLOCKS?

GIDEON! WHAT ABOUT MOTHER'S DYING WISH? IS THE FAULT THE FAIRCHILL THAT SHE DIED—!

I WILL WITNESS AGAINST YOU AT THE COUNCIL. I WILL REVEAL WHAT GOES ON HERE AT NIGHT. I WILL TELL THEM THAT YOU ARE WORKING FOR MORTMAIN. I WILL TELL THEM WHY.

THAT IS A LIE. SHE TOOK HER OWN LIFE, BUT NOT BECAUSE OF ANYTHING MY FATHER DID. IT WAS RATHER BECAUSE OF SOMETHING YOUR FATHER DID.

FATHER—?

BE QUIET, GABRIEL.

WITHDRAW YOUR CLAIM ON THE INSTITUTE. SPEAK OUT FOR CHARLOTTE IN FRONT OF THE COUNCIL.

I KNOW BLACKMAIL WHEN I HEAR IT, CHARLOTTE. WHAT DO YOU WANT FROM ME?

HE WILL HAVE THE CLAVE.

I COMMUNICATED WITH HIM THROUGH NATHANIEL GRAY, BUT YOU KILLED HIM.

WE NEED TO KNOW HOW YOU HAVE BEEN COMMUNICATING WITH MORTMAIN, AND WHERE HE IS.

BUT I'M JUST ONE OF HIS MANY PLANS, A STRAND OF HIS WEB.

AND HE WILL HAVE HER.

WHAT DOES HE INTEND TO DO WITH ME?

I DON'T KNOW. I DO KNOW HE WAS CONSISTENTLY ASKING AFTER YOUR WELFARE. SUCH CONCERN, SO TOUCHING IN A POTENTIAL BRIDEGROOM.

AND GIDEON, UNDERSTAND THAT IF YOU SUPPORT CHARLOTTE BRANWELL IN THIS, YOU WILL NO LONGER BE WELCOME UNDER MY ROOF.

......

CLINK

GABRIEL, COME WITH ME.

...I WILL STAY AND TAKE CARE OF FATHER.

GIDEON...

BUT...I...

I TRUST WE WILL SEE YOU TOMORROW IN THE COUNCIL CHAMBER, BENEDICT. I ALSO TRUST YOU WILL KNOW WHAT TO DO.

CLIP-CLOP

CLIP-CLOP

I TRIED TO MAKE YOU HATE ME, BUT THEN I WANTED TO DIE. AFTER THAT NIGHT ON THE ROOF, I WENT TO MAGNUS, TO ASK FOR HELP.

THERE IS NO CURSE ON ME, TESSA. THE DEMON TRICKED ME. THERE NEVER WAS A CURSE. ALL THESE YEARS, I'VE BEEN A FOOL.

I KNOW THAT YOU HAVE NO REASON TO GIVE ME A SECOND CHANCE TO BE REGARDED BY YOU IN A DIFFERENT LIGHT.

BUT I AM BEGGING YOU FOR THAT CHANCE. I WILL DO ANYTHING. *ANYTHING.*

WILL, NO. IT'S TOO LATE. IT ISN'T... POSSIBLE.

IT IS. IT MUST BE. YOU CANNOT HATE ME AS MUCH AS ALL THAT—

JEM HAS PROPOSED TO ME.

AND I HAVE SAID YES.

THE INFERNAL DEVICES
CLOCKWORK PRINCE

SO WE
ARE HERE
TODAY...

CHAPTER 16

AS THE GREAT MUNDANE MILITARY STRATEGIST SUN TZU SAID "IF YOU KNOW YOUR ENEMIES AND KNOW YOURSELF, YOU CAN WIN A HUNDRED BATTLES WITHOUT A SINGLE LOSS."

WE KNOW NOW WHO MORTMAIN REALLY IS—A MORTAL MAN WHO UTILIZED WEREWOLVES TO HELP HIM BUILD HIS CLOCKWORK ARMY. JUDGING BY THE SIZE OF THE WAREHOUSE HE USED, HIS ARMY WILL BE SIZEABLE.

AND JUDGING BY THE YEARS HE HAS PLANNED, HE IS A MAN WHO CANNOT BE REASONED WITH. WE MUST PREPARE FOR A WAR.

PREPARE HOW?

WELL, ALLYING OURSELVES WITH SOME OF DOWNWORLD'S MORE POWERFUL LEADERS LIKE WOOLSEY SCOTT AND CAMILLE BELCOURT WILL HELP. CHARLOTTE SEEMS TO HAVE THEM ALL WELL IN HAND, DON'T YOU THINK?

AND ABOUT THE SPY, CHARLOTTE DEALT WITH THE MATTER SWIFTLY AND WITHOUT COMPASSION. I RETRACT MY EARLIER STATEMENT ABOUT HER SOFTHEARTEDNESS. CLEARLY SHE IS AS ABLE TO DEAL JUSTICE WITHOUT PITY AS ANY MAN.

I WISH YOU HAD COME TO THIS CONCLUSION A FORTNIGHT AGO, BENEDICT, AND SAVED US ALL THIS TROUBLE.

EITHER WAY, LET US VOTE ON IT.

Charlotte
Brannell

YES!!

LOOK!!

Bzzzzt

Bzzzzt

Bzzzzt

Bzzzzt

I THOUGHT I WOULD WAKE UP THIS MORNING AND IT WOULD HAVE BEEN A DREAM, YOU SAYING YES TO ME. BUT IT WASN'T.

I'M SORRY YOU'RE GETTING SUCH A BAD BARGAIN IN ME, TESSA. SHACKLING YOURSELF TO A DYING MAN WHEN YOU'RE ONLY SIXTEEN...

YOU'RE ONLY SEVENTEEN. PLENTY OF TIME TO FIND A CURE.

AND WE WILL. FIND ONE.

I WILL BE WITH YOU.

FOREVER.

WE WERE BEGINNING TO WONDER WHERE YOU TWO WERE—

TESSA AND I HAVE NEWS.

WELL, TELL US!

TESSA AND I ARE ENGAGED TO BE MARRIED.

I ASKED HER, AND—SHE ACCEPTED ME.

SHOULDN'T YOU TELL THEM...MORE CAREFULLY?

WELL, I HAVE NEWS OF MY OWN. GOOD NEWS.

HENRY AND I ARE GOING TO HAVE A CHILD. A BOY.

WHAT?!

DARLING, THAT'S WONDERFUL, WONDERFUL!

MY DARLING, YOU MUST REMAIN ABED FOR THE NEXT EIGHT MONTHS. LITTLE BUFORD—

I AM NOT NAMING OUR CHILD BUFORD!

MR. BRANWELL, THERE'S SOMEONE HERE TO SEE YOU ALL.

SOMEONE TO SEE US? BUT THIS IS A PRIVATE DINNER, CYRIL.

SHE IS NEPHILIM.

AND SHE SAYS IT'S VERY IMPORTANT.

TO BE CONTINUED

THE INFERNAL DEVICES: CLOCKWORK PRINCE

CASSANDRA CLARE
HYEKYUNG BAEK

Art and Adaptation: HyeKyung Baek

Lettering: JuYoun Lee

Text copyright © Cassandra Claire, LLC 2011

Illustrations © Hachette Book Group, Inc.

Yen Press
Hachette Book Group
237 Park Avenue, New York, NY 10017

www.HachetteBookGroup.com
www.YenPress.com

Yen Press is an imprint of Hachette Book Group, Inc. The Yen Press name and logo are trademarks of Hachette Book Group, Inc.

First Yen Press Edition: September 2013

ISBN: 978-0-316-20096-7

10 9 8 7 6 5 4 3 2 1

BVG

Printed in the United States of America